SHARKS
IN DANGER

by Paul Mason

HUNGRY TOMATO™

CONTENTS

HUMANS V. SHARKS

Most of us are scared of sharks, but there is no real reason why we should be. Only a tiny number of people each year are attacked by sharks.

WHALE SHARK

For the sharks, it is a different story. Sharks have very good reason to be scared of humans. We kill millions of sharks a year. Almost all are from species that are no danger to humans.

The exact numbers are changing all the time, but the International Union for Conservation of Nature (IUCN) says that:

- About 10 different types of shark are **critically endangered**. They are soon likely to become **extinct** in the wild.

- Roughly 15 types of shark are **endangered**, including great hammerheads. There is a strong possibility that they will soon disappear from our seas.

- Close to 40 different species of shark are **vulnerable**, including whale sharks and great whites. This means they may become extinct in a few years' time, if action is not taken.

We shouldn't be scared OF sharks.
We should be scared FOR them.

Critically endangered sharks in 2017 included the:

ANGEL SHARK
Mediterranean, north-eastern Atlantic
The angel shark, smoothback angel shark and sawback angel shark are all threatened by **overfishing**.

DAGGERNOSE SHARK
Northern South America
Fishing is thought to reduce the number of daggernose sharks by 18 per cent each year. It took just 10 years for over 90% of the population to be wiped out.

GANGES SHARK
India
This river shark is threatened by overfishing and pollution. It is also losing **habitat** as dams are built on the rivers where it lives.

IRRAWADDY RIVER SHARK
Myanmar
The **mangrove** forests where this shark hunts are steadily being cut down. The rivers it lives in have also become polluted.

NEW GUINEA RIVER SHARK
Northern Australia, possibly New Guinea
Threatened by overfishing, there are thought to be only about 250 of these sharks left.

PONDICHERRY SHARK
China, India, Indonesia, Malaysia, Oman, Pakistan
Last caught and identified by experts in 1979, this species may now actually be extinct.

NATAL SHYSHARK
South Africa
This shark lives close to the coast in a very small area of Kwa-Zulu Natal, where industry and development are threatening its habitat.

A whale shark swims along, gathering small sea creatures into its giant mouth as it goes.

WHO NEEDS SHARKS ANYWAY?

We ALL need sharks. They are a crucial part of life in our oceans. If sharks disappear, the balance of the ocean world is upset.

APEX PREDATORS

Many sharks are apex predators. This means that they are not usually hunted by any other animal. If the number of apex predators declines, it harms the natural environment. The examples on this page and opposite show how this can happen.

Tiger sharks are apex predators. Seabirds are part of their diet.

If the tiger shark population falls, the number of seabirds goes up.

Tuna numbers fall, affecting fish such as marlin that feed on tuna.

Seabirds eat young tuna. If there are more seabirds, more young tuna get eaten.

Fewer young tuna then grow up to replace older fish as they die.

SHARKS AND SCALLOPS

On the Atlantic coast of the USA, shark numbers have recently fallen because of overfishing. This has led to an increase in cow-nose rays, which the sharks would normally eat. Cow-nose rays love scallops, a tasty shellfish, so with more cow-nose rays there are fewer scallops.

SHARKS AND REEFS

Experts have discovered that having sharks around helps keep coral reefs healthy. When shark numbers fall, fewer large fish, such as grouper, are eaten. More grouper eat smaller fish such as parrot fish. Parrot fish are important for keeping the reef healthy, because they eat algae. Without enough parrot fish to eat algae, the reef becomes choked with algae and unhealthy.

SHARK SCIENCE: FOOD CHAIN

A food chain is a group of living things that depend on each other for food. At the bottom are small plants and animals. These are eaten by other animals. They in turn are eaten by larger, fiercer predators. At the top of the food chain are the apex predators.

SHARK FINNING

The practice of catching a shark and cutting off its fins is called shark finning. The fins are used in shark fin soup. The soup is a favourite dish in Asia, especially China.

WIPING OUT THE WORLD'S SHARKS

Shark finning is wiping out the world's sharks. In some seas, so many have been killed that only 1 per cent of the population is left.

Experts worked out that, in 2006, about 38 million sharks were killed by the shark fin industry. For the same number of people to die, you would have to kill the entire populations of Switzerland, London, Rio de Janeiro, Sydney, New York City and Los Angeles – every year.

Experts believe that shark numbers have fallen by more than half since the 1980s as a result of demand for shark fin soup.

First the shark is caught, either on a hook or in a net.

Then the shark's tail, dorsal and pectoral fins are cut off. It is almost always still alive when this happens.

The shark is tipped back into the sea, usually still alive. Without fins it cannot swim.

The shark sinks to the sea bottom and either bleeds to death, is eaten by other sea creatures, or suffocates.

AGAINST SHARK FINNING

The trade in fins has been banned in many places. Some hotels and restaurants will not serve shark fin soup, and some airlines refuse to transport the fins. It has also become clear that shark fins can contain dangerous levels of mercury, which is harmful to humans (see page 15). As a result, demand for the fins has fallen in Hong Kong – the world's main trading place for shark fins.

Shark fins are dried and bleached (right), before being sold and becoming the main ingredient of shark fin soup (above).

SHARK SCIENCE:
SHARK SUFFOCATION

Sharks whose fins have been cut off suffocate because they cannot swim. Sharks usually breathe by taking oxygen from water flowing over their **gills**. If the shark cannot swim, there is no water flow. The shark doesn't get oxygen and slowly suffocates.

BIG-GAME AND COMMERCIAL FISHING

Sharks are not only caught for their fins. Some types of shark are caught for fun by 'big-game fishermen'. Sharks are also caught so that their meat can be sold.

MAKO SHARK

BIG-GAME FISHING

Catching large, powerful fish using a strong rod and reel is known as big-game fishing. People enjoy the challenge of battling against a fish that is fighting for its life. Mako sharks are popular targets among big-game fishermen. Makos fight hard and make spectacular leaps into the air as they try to escape. Great whites, blue, tiger and bull sharks are also sometimes caught.

CATCH AND RELEASE

As the phrase suggests, 'catch and release' is catching a fish, then letting it go. Today it is becoming popular with big-game fishermen. Although the fish is sometimes too exhausted to live, many fish do seem to survive. Overall, fewer sharks and other fish are killed.

COMMERCIAL FISHING

When fishermen catch sharks for their meat, they usually aim to catch particular species. For example:

- Around the north-eastern Atlantic Ocean, a type of shark called spiny dogfish is caught. It is renamed 'rock salmon', 'flake' or 'huss', then sold in fish and chip shops.

- Salmon shark hearts are a delicacy in Japan, as are gulper shark eggs in the Maldives.

- Greenland or basking sharks are caught and **putrefied** to make 'hákarl', a national dish of Iceland.

In some parts of the world, commercial fishing is having a disastrous effect on shark numbers. All the sharks above are **under threat**, and in some places the spiny dogfish is critically endangered.

Spiny dogfish

Greenland shark

SHARK SCIENCE:
CATCH AND RELEASE SURVIVAL

Scientists can observe what happens to a shark that has been caught and released in two ways:

1) By taking a sample of its blood – chemicals in the blood show how the fish has been affected by being caught. Many are completely exhausted

2) By fitting a 'pinger'– its signal shows whether the fish is still moving around and therefore alive

By-catch

Fishermen often catch sharks in their nets without intending to. This is called 'by-catch'. By-catch is usually put back in the sea, dead or dying.

As this shark struggled to escape, it became more and more wrapped up in the net. Eventually it suffocated.

Drift gill nets

Drift gill nets produce a lot of by-catch. They are fishing nets that hang down in the water like a curtain. When fish swim into the net they become trapped. They cannot swim forwards, and cannot escape because their gills become caught up. The nets accidentally trap many sharks, as well as turtles, dolphins and even small whales.

Longlining

Longlining is an alternative to using drift gill nets. It makes it easier to catch exactly the right kind of fish.

A long, strong fishing line is released into the water. Dangling from the line are baited hooks, which hang at the depth where the target fish usually swim. The size of hook and bait are also designed to attract the right catch. Some unwanted fish do still get hooked, but fewer than those caught in drift nets.

This Alaskan halibut was caught on a longline set up specifically to catch this kind of fish.

QUOTAS

In many parts of the world, fishing boats have quotas. These are the set amounts of fish that may be caught. The quota usually specifies that the boat can catch only certain types and sizes of fish. Anything else must be thrown back. This produces a lot of by-catch.

Recently, some governments have started using a different kind of quota. The boats are allowed to keep any fish they catch. The only limit is the overall weight. The aim is to stop sharks and other fish being caught, killed and dumped in the sea.

SHARK SCIENCE: SHARK POISON

Eating a lot of shark meat is not only bad for the ocean environment. It can also be bad for your health.

The reason is that the flesh of large sharks sometimes contains a chemical called methylmercury. This harms the human nervous system and can even cause brain damage.

PROTECTIVE NETTING

Very few humans are ever attacked by sharks. In some places, though, sharks make it dangerous for swimmers and surfers. Here, large nets are sometimes used to keep people safe.

This young tiger shark became trapped in a protective net and died.

HARMFUL NETS

The nets are deadly to sharks and other large sea creatures. They do not simply force sharks to turn away – they trap them in the same way as drift nets (see page 14). And few of those sharks caught in nets belong to species that have attacked humans. Harmless sea creatures such as turtles also get caught in the nets.

SHARK CULLS

When shark attacks happen, people sometimes demand a **cull** of dangerous sharks. After a series of attacks in Western Australia in 2014, a cull of large predatory sharks was announced. But many people felt that the sharks would be killed without cause. After pro-shark demonstrations, the authorities cancelled the cull.

People demonstrate against a planned shark cull in Western Australia. After the cull was cancelled, experts from South Africa came to advise on setting up a shark-spotting scheme (see page 17).

SHARK SPOTTERS

On some beaches that once had shark nets, an alternative system is now being used. In South Africa, shark spotters watch from high ground, using powerful binoculars to look for sharks. If they see one, they radio the beach. A warning siren goes off and everyone knows to leave the water.

On South Africa's Cape Peninsula, a flag system warns swimmers and surfers about the risk of shark attacks:

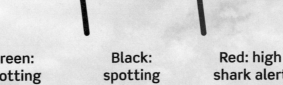

Green: spotting conditions are good

Black: spotting conditions are poor

Red: high shark alert

White: a shark has been spotted, leave the water (a warning siren also goes off)

In summer, Shark Beach in Sydney Harbour, Australia, is protected by a shark net.

SHARK SCIENCE: SHOCKING SHARKS

Sharks can sense the tiny electric charges given off by their prey. They use this in the final stages of an attack.

One company has developed an anti-shark attack device that gives off pulses of electricity. If a shark comes too close, the electric pulses confuse it and make it turn away.

SHARK TOURISM

Lots of people are fascinated by sharks, so trips to see them are popular. 'Shark tourism' is not always good for the sharks, but it can bring big benefits.

DIVE TOURISM

Diving with sharks in their natural habitat is a great way to get really close to them. The shark-diving industry is worth hundreds of millions of dollars a year. To make sure there are plenty of sharks for tourists to see, several countries have set up areas where shark fishing is banned. As a result, few sharks are killed there.

CAGE DIVING

Cage diving uses a steel cage that floats just below the surface. Divers inside the cage are safe from attack, so this is a popular way to see dangerous sharks. The organizers sometimes put blood and bait in the water to attract the sharks. Some surfers and swimmers say this can lead to more attacks, and that it makes sharks connect humans with blood and food.

BOAT TOURISM

Almost all sharks are harmless – but most shark fans still prefer to see them from the safety of a boat. This is causing problems for some species, especially large sharks. Whale sharks in particular are damaged by boats, when parties of tourists are brought too close.

SHARK SCIENCE:
WHALE SHARK GATHERINGS

Whale sharks generally roam the world's oceans alone. Sometimes, though, many gather together in one place to feed.

The biggest gathering is off the coast of Yucatán, Mexico. In some years, the hatching of millions of tiny tuna attracts the whale sharks. In 2009, over 400 of the sharks were seen in a single day.

SHARK REPRODUCTION

Many sharks do not reproduce very quickly. This means not enough baby sharks are being born to replace the millions of adult sharks that are killed each year.

REACHING MATURITY

Most sharks take a long time to reach **maturity.** Fortunately, they do not all take as long as the Greenland shark to have young – 100 years or more! Even a female great white, though, will be over 30 years old before she has pups (newborn sharks).

LONG PREGNANCIES

When sharks do start to have young, it takes a long time for the baby sharks to arrive. Female sharks are usually pregnant for 9–12 months. Many then wait two years before reproducing again.

SMALL LITTERS

A group of young sharks born together is called a litter. Sharks usually have small litters. The bigeye thresher shark, for example, has only two pups at a time. Even the blue shark, which has the biggest litters, has only about 135. This is a tiny number compared to other fish. The bluefin tuna, for example, produces up to 10 million eggs a year, although only a fraction of these survive.

A dogfish, or lesser spotted shark, hatches from an egg – often called a 'mermaid's purse'.

The sand tiger shark will eat young sharks if it can catch them.

A DANGEROUS WORLD

For newborn sharks, the world is a more dangerous place than ever. There a fewer safe nursery areas (see page 22), and many young sharks end up as by-catch in fishing nets. This means that fewer sharks reach an age where they can reproduce. Overall, shark numbers fall as a result.

SHARK SCIENCE: SHARK PERFUME

Many sharks are solitary and may be far away from a possible mate. When they are ready to breed, female sharks release special chemicals into the water. If a male shark from the same species gets a sniff of this perfume, it heads in the female's direction.

21

SHARK NURSERIES

A nursery is a place where young sharks spend time while they are growing up. The youngsters are not very good at defending themselves, so the nursery has to be somewhere safe.

ESTUARIES AND MANGROVES

Many sharks have their young in shallow-water nurseries, where there are plenty of places to hide from larger predators. The young sharks also need a supply of small fish to eat (as shown here). Estuaries – the mouths of rivers where the water is salty – make good shark nurseries. There are often weeds and other plants, rocks and piers that provide shelter. Mangrove forests are also places of safety. The baby sharks can hide – and hunt – among the tangled mangrove roots.

Space is tight among the mangrove roots. When baby sharks grow larger, it is time for them to move on.

This blacktip reef shark cruising through the mangroves is a youngster. When it grows larger, it will hunt further out to sea.

This hornshark egg case has a beautiful spiral shape.

Threats to shark nurseries

One problem for sharks is that their nurseries are slowly disappearing. Estuaries are often very beautiful, so they are popular places for people to live. Each year, more new homes and marinas are built along estuaries. Around the world, mangrove forests are also cut down to make way for shrimp farms and salt farms.

If their nurseries continue to disappear, shark numbers will fall even if humans stop killing millions of sharks each year. With fewer safe places, more young sharks will die before they reach adulthood.

SHARK SCIENCE: HATCHED OR BORN

Baby sharks arrive in the world in two different ways. Some hatch from eggs laid by the mother. The eggs are often shaped to be wedged into narrow spaces, where predators cannot reach them.

Most sharks develop inside their mother and are born ready to swim off. These mini-predators are ready to start hunting right away. But because they are so small, they are also a tasty snack for other predators, so few make it to adulthood.

OCEAN POLLUTION

For many years, humans have been polluting the sea with chemicals and waste. This ocean pollution is making it harder for sharks to survive.

Tags enable scientists to monitor sharks and their movements.

Off the state of New Jersey, USA, shortfin mako sharks have been found to contain dangerous levels of the chemical methylmercury.

CHEMICAL POLLUTION

Each year, more of our chemicals get into the sea. For example, farm fertilizers are washed off the land by rain and flow into rivers. The rivers carry these chemicals to the sea.

Some of the chemicals are toxic (poisonous). Sharks found with these substances in their bodies include:

- Young great whites with high levels of DDT, a poisonous chemical that affects the shark's ability to breathe and the flow of blood around its body
- Greenland sharks with large amounts of PCBs (chemicals banned in the USA in 1979, and internationally in 2001); PCBs may affect the shark's health, including its ability to reproduce and the development of young sharks
- Sharks with mercury and lead contamination: their flesh has up to 10 times the levels considered safe to eat

Some areas of the seabed off California contain large amounts of the toxic chemical DDT. The DDT has been there since the 1970s and is still being **absorbed** by fish – including sharks.

SHORTFIN MAKO SHARK

CARBON DIOXIDE

Today, our oceans contain increasing amounts of carbon dioxide. This is affecting sharks and other sea life. Scientists are not certain what the long-term effects will be. There is some evidence that it makes it harder for sharks to smell prey. They change their hunting patterns and swim long distances looking for cleaner water.

SHARK SCIENCE: CARBON DIOXIDE IN THE OCEANS

Oceans absorb carbon dioxide from the air. The amount in the air is increasing. In 1950, it was already the highest ever: just over 300 parts per million. Since then, it has risen to over 400 parts per million.

The extra carbon dioxide came from burning fossil fuels: coal, oil and natural gas. These fuels contain carbon dioxide. When they are burned, it is released into the air.

The catshark has been used to study how carbon dioxide affects shark behaviour.

SAVING OUR SHARKS

Although finning and other threats are making life very difficult for sharks, things are not all bad. Recently, there have been some changes that will help protect them.

This reef shark has been tagged by a Caribbean shark research project. The simple tag will allow scientists to identify the shark if they come across it again.

UNDERSTANDING SHARKS

Publicity for sharks can play a big part in saving them. It helps people understand that sharks are crucial to the life of our oceans. For example, one of the best-known sharks is the great white. As the understanding of this shark has increased, more people have become interested in its **conservation**. Great white numbers are now rising. In 2009, just five great whites were spotted off the coast of Cape Cod, USA. By 2014 it was 80. Two years later, the number had risen to 147.

The fight against finning

Finning is the biggest single threat to sharks. In 2013, countries around the world agreed to restrict trade in oceanic whitetip, porbeagle and three hammerhead species. Also in 2013, the EU banned shark finning by its boats anywhere in the world. Elsewhere in 2015, laws were confirmed to ban trade in shark fins in 10 US states. The following year, the state of Rhode Island also banned the trade in shark fins.

Net hazards

Steps have been taken to stop so many sharks being accidentally caught in nets. On many beaches, shark nets are being replaced by shark spotters. Out at sea, fishermen sometimes use large floating objects to attract fish. If these are made with netting, they can entangle sharks. New net-free versions prevent this happening.

Shark science: SHARKS ONLINE

You no longer have to follow a shark in real life to know what it is up to. Some sharks have their own social media!

Several great whites have been tagged with GPS devices. News of where they are goes out on their Twitter accounts. For example, great whites @MaryLeeShark and @RockStarLydia regularly tweet 'their' news and views.

SEVEN INCREDIBLE SHARK FACTS

1 **You would be REALLY unlucky to be bitten by a shark**

Most victims of shark attacks are surfers. Even so, a surfer in California (where some of the most serious attacks have taken place) has a one-in-17-million chance of being bitten. They are actually more likely to win the lottery.

2 **Humans kill over 100,000 sharks a day for their fins...**

...that's 4,000 sharks every hour, or 66.6 sharks every minute. So we kill at least one shark a second, every second of every day of the year.

3 **Shark fins are a multi-million-dollar industry**

Most sharks are killed for their fins, which can sell for over £770 ($1,000) per kilogram. They are used in a soup that is a traditional dish at Chinese weddings and New Year celebrations. In restaurants, a single bowl can cost over £150 ($200).

4 **Shark fins don't taste of much**

You cannot taste the fin in shark fin soup. It is added because of how it feels to crunch or chew on. Shark fins also have no **nutritional** value, so eating them really does seem pointless.

5 SHARKS HAVE AMAZING IMMUNE SYSTEMS

Scientists are uncertain just how a shark's **immune system** works, but it does seem to be very effective. Sharks are rarely ill. Studying shark immune systems may one day help human medicine.

6 A SINGLE (LIVE) SHARK CAN BE WORTH NEARLY £1.5 MILLION

In Palau, an island in the Pacific Ocean, reef sharks live in places where divers can almost always see them. Shark tourists spend so much money in Palau that, in its 16-year life, a single shark could be worth nearly £1.5 million ($2 million) to the local economy. No wonder Palau declared itself the world's first shark sanctuary in 2009.

7 THERE ARE 15 SHARK SANCTUARIES AROUND THE WORLD

By 2017, shark fishing had been banned in 15 areas around the world. These shark sancturies are all in the south-west Pacific Ocean or near the Caribbean Sea.

VISITING WITH SHARKS

Some aquariums have sharks you can watch swimming around. But for a true shark fan, nothing beats the thrill of seeing sharks swimming in the wild. Here are some of the top places to do that – and remember always to go with a responsible, licensed operator.

USA
From June to November, shortfin mako sharks head for southern California in search of food. This is one of the best places to spot these amazing predators. They are often seen swimming near blue sharks, also common in the area.

BAHAMAS
Bimini in the Bahamas is home to the Bimini Shark Lab. The area is famous for bull sharks and hammerheads. This is a great place to see sharks in the wild and to find out about the Lab's shark conservation research.

FIJI
Fiji's Beqa Lagoon is a prime shark-diving location, but this is not a place for the nervous! The sharks here include bull sharks, tigers and large lemon sharks – as well as less scary whitetip and blacktip reef sharks.

MEXICO
Mexico's Yucután Peninsula boasts all kinds of sea life, including humpback whales and whale sharks (see page 19).

COSTA RICA
Cocos Island, off Costa Rica, is known for huge schools of hundreds of scalloped hammerheads. Divers can regularly watch the hammerheads, as well as whitetip reef sharks.

SOUTH AFRICA
Great whites swim the seas of the Cape region, while the Aliwal Shoal, off KwaZulu-Natal, is a breeding ground for sand tiger sharks. Whale sharks can be seen off South Africa's north-east coast.

MALDIVES
The Maldive islands are surrounded by warm, shallow sea, perfect for marine life. Maaya Thila is a protected marine environment where divers often swim with whitetip reef sharks and other sea creatures.

AUSTRALIA
The Neptune Islands, off South Australia, are famous for great white sharks. Visitors can dive with Shark Expeditions, founded by Rodney Fox, a great white expert and conservationist.

GLOSSARY

absorb
take in or soak up through the surface and into the inside

conservation
keeping the natural world safe, so that animals and environments do not disappear

critically endangered
the International Union of Conservation for Nature (IUCN) category for species facing an extremely high risk of extinction

cull
deliberate killing of animals to reduce their population

endangered
the International Union of Conservation for Nature (IUCN) category for species facing a high risk of extinction

extinct
without a single living example

gill
body part that allows a fish to breathe; the gills take oxygen from water in the same way human lungs take oxygen from air

habitat
natural home of a plant or animal

immune system
body system that allows living things to fight off disease

mangrove
a type of tree that grows along the edge of salty water in hot places

maturity
age when a living thing is physically able to produce young

nutritional
providing the ingredients needed for health and growth

overfishing
catching so many fish that their number drops to dangerously low levels, so they cannot be replaced

pollution
harming or poisoning an environment with toxic substances and materials

putrefied
allowed to rot

tag
identification label, which may give off a signal so the shark can be tracked

under threat
general term for species that face some kind of danger to their survival

vulnerable
the International Union of Conservation for Nature (IUCN) category for species that will become endangered if their situation does not improve

INDEX

About the author

Paul Mason is a prolific author of children's books, many award-nominated, on such subjects as 101 ways to save the planet, vile things that go wrong with the human body, and the world's looniest inventors. Many take off via surprising, unbelievable or just plain revolting facts. Today, he lives at a secret location on the coast of Europe, where his writing shack usually smells of drying wetsuit (he's a former international swimmer and a keen surfer).

Picture Credits
(abbreviations: t = top; b = bottom; c = centre; l = left; r = right)
Alamy: Alessandro Mancini 25br; David Angel 16; Design Pics Inc 15t; Doug Perrine 8cl; Erika Antoniazzo 11r; Ger Bosma 9t; Image Source 12; Jeff Rotman 16tl; Kevin Browne 25tl; Mark Conlin 8bl; NATUREWORLD 8c; Reinhard Dirscherl 18bl; Top Photo Corporation 11cl; WaterFrame 3, 13cr, 20tl; Wolfgang Polzer 21tl. FLPA: Christian Ziegler/Minden Pictures 22bl; Colin Marshall 19tl; Jean-Michel Mille/Biosphoto 20; John Holmes 8; MICHAEL WEBERBERGER/Imagebroker 32br; Norbert Wu/Minden Pictures 1, 2, 22, 6, 14, 23tr, 28t; OceanPhoto 9c; Pete Oxford/Minden Pictures 26; Peter Verhoog/Minden Pictures 29b; Photo Researchers 18; Steve Trewhella 13tr; Suzi Eszterhas/ Minden Pictures 28. Getty Images: Matt Jelonek 16b.